Cover art by Erech Overaker
Layout by Zac Smith
Additional copyediting by Alan Good

Typeset in Baskerville

ISBN: 978-1-7332757-6-7

Watertown

Dan Eastman

You're long and lean
But things don't get you down
You're a top ten kingpin in the borders
Of your hometown

– *The Tragically Hip, "Small Town Bringdown"*

Watertown

Table of Contents

The Nice Side of Watertown

Every year, my wife and I visit Watertown. She humors me in the reluctant way spouses are obligated to do – like it would be rude to kick someone out of the party when they show up uninvited so you pretend to be happy they're here. That's how my wife is about Watertown. We stay with my mom in her house on the corner with the wood panel walls among the overgrown lawns and smoked-out homes in stages of disrepair. I drive the long way around town to show her there's actually a nice side to Watertown: a neighborhood tucked away with pastel vinyl and fresh-painted wooden porches, places where the snow never browns to sludge in the winter. I want to show her it can be good.

"One of my friends lived here growing up. He had a tennis court in his backyard," I say. "This is the nice side of Watertown." I've lost count how many times I've said it over how many visits. Slowing the car to a crawl, we see it. The net is drooping and somehow the green court is now the color of rust.

She looks at the dried-up grass, at the yellow dog piss spots. "I still don't see it."

blinking yellow pixels in the distance behind a pale curtain

snowbound traffic
craggy face in neon vest
writing poetry with a red flag
words
carried

off

in a blizzard

Watertown

yes, these poems
are about a place
but they're also about
loving something
in spite of its flaws
loving something
in a way no one else can
and loving something
that will never love you back

Upstate

New York is New York City
everything else is Upstate

Trivia

In 1970 during
a career low point
Frank Sinatra released
Watertown.

A concept album
about lovers leaving
and train tracks
and factories.

Frank Sinatra had never
even visited Watertown
but you might say
Watertown visited him.

Time Warp

1.

there's a local myth
about a time warp
in the woods
at Thompson Park
overlooking
Watertown
once inside
you relive
pivotal moments
of your life.
writing poems
works too
I guess.

2.

to attract visitors
they put up a sign
in the park
that says
Watertown's Area 51
and just like that
all the magic
was gone.

We've Got 100 Words for Snow and Most of Them Are "Fuck"

wind-whipped through a blanket of snow feeling the burning on my face and telling the snow to go fuck itself. in the same breath I say I love you, snow. seeing a pear-shaped woman shovel a huge boulder, stumbled and drop it. same woman smashing her shovel on the sidewalk. the utter futility of getting mad at the weather. cresting a bank and holing up for a moment inside the Byrne Dairy gas station. pulling my swollen hands from my pockets to find they've formed a perfect curve. flesh carved from wood. hands perfectly curved for cradling a paper coffee cup and the pain makes sense like it always finds a way to do. hands becoming branches splintering in a climate they weren't made for. and I sink into a booth watching the blank outside. flakes hit the windows like gravel spit up behind truck tires. glad for the pain melding into loneliness becoming a sort of warmth, you know the kind. rigs coming and going some stuck spinning in banks going nowhere at all. I beg them come inside with me with me and my frozen hook hands

Brief Wins Living Out of a Ford Escort and Sleeping on Dirty Apartment Floors

I have never felt
more like a champion
than after finally scraping
enough pennies
off a sticky coffee table
to afford a $1.39 burrito
from Taco Bell
on a Saturday afternoon.
I am Stone Cold Steven Austin
giving everyone the finger
after winning the title
from Shawn Michaels
at *Wrestlemania XII*.
Traffic on the narrowest
two lane highways
will part for me today.

Wealthy Prospects

Now
whenever I feel depressed
I recall a time
when offers of
$8 an hour
in a retail chain
felt like
wealthy prospects.

Viggo Mortensen

1.

went to high school in Watertown
and sometimes he comes back
so all my friends have Viggo stories

my friend Sam saw Viggo
getting gas
at Byrne Dairy

Ryan saw Viggo
working out
at the Y

I've never seen Viggo
but it occurs to me
that I can just say I did

no one would ever doubt me

2.

my friends and I were at the bar
the one owned by the mayor
when I decided to tell them
I saw Viggo Mortensen
only I was thinking about the movie *Eastern
  Promises*
when I said
I saw Viggo Mortensen's balls

Black River

Ambling stoned across
rocks on the river's edge
rapids flushing out trash and rafters
we step over rusty Pepsi cans
stumble through
the weeds and the brush
burdocks sticking to Billabong sweatshirts
I envy the way you stay upright
before coolly sinking into
the cigarette-burned
seats of a used Civic
looking for a decent spot
in the parking lot of life
somewhere close to the entrance
I am going to remember this
in ten years when
you Facebook message me
about how the vitamins you're selling
are going to totally change the way
I think about nutrition.
Thanks.

Public Square

well
it's more of a circle
than a square
and most of the windows
are covered
with plywood
which is square

Public Square 2

there's a statue
of an angel
in Public Square

one time someone
crashed their car
into the statue

another time
some kids stole the statue
the whole heavy-ass thing

Watertown keeps replacing
the angel statue
truly believing
each one is the last

that's the spirit
now
let's go steal a fuckin statue

Dad

the greatest memory
with my dad
is the one where
we are sitting
in a rowboat
in the middle
of Lake Ontario
nothing is said
and nothing needs
to be said
no pressure
tiny waves
swish swashing
around the boat
and the infinite
horizon
of the lake.
also
this never happened.

Grownup Soup

When I was eight I fell in love with ship watching. Dad's buddy Pat had a cottage on the St. Lawrence River where they stayed for long weekends hunting in the woods. I told my dad I wanted to go just for those cold mornings alone. Awake before anyone else, my gaze gravitated between an *Elvira: Mistress of the Dark* tape and the large barges passing under the gargantuan green bridge of the Seaway. I didn't give a shit about hunting. I just thought cargo ships were badass.

Steel mammoths powered their way through untamed waters. Drinking the river and shitting it out. Sick.

In the yard at Pat's cottage sat a lighthouse so small. Too small. No way those ships could've seen its signal. Had to have been a gnome that worked it. One determined morning I crept out in my Spider-Man pajamas, wet grass under my toes, fish stink in the air. I was going to peel back a slab of wood and peek inside. See exactly how this thing worked. I got to the lighthouse and suddenly one of the barges farted. Startled, I pussied out and darted back to the TV under the flannel blanket and fixed sights on Elvira's exposed thigh. Waves rolled against the rocky shore telling me to shush.

The coffee pot gargled on auto and the river glistened under new sun.

Unshaven in Carhartt jackets and denim, Dad and Pat ambled downstairs for Maxwell House.

Phlegm roiled in their throats the way real men announce their presence in the morning. We took the truck to the woods. I sat in the middle seat between them, sinking low as the boredom set in. Dry leaves and twigs crackled underfoot. We were supposed to blend in with the browning autumn trees as we scouted something to kill. I couldn't take my eyes off the sleek black Swiss-cheese barrel of Pat's gun. It was something from a movie.

"It's so cool," I said. I thought sparks might fly out of it with a hailstorm of bullets.

He gave me a closer look. I looked eye to eye with it, peering down the infinite darkness of the barrel.

"How'd you like to catch one from this thing?" Pat asked with a chuckle. "Huh-huh-huh-huh." His laugh kind of reminded me of Butt-Head of Beavis and Butt-Head fame, which made the cool gun even more sick. Dad shot us both a shut the fuck up glare as if he saw something. But there wasn't anything out there. He just knew Pat's gun was cooler than his old Remington.

No deer. No kill. Nothing would die on that day. No sons became men.

Rocks ting-tinged on the bottom of the truck. A cold Thermos in the cupholder. "Can I have some soup?" Pat laughed. "That's grownup soup." Then he belched loudly over the sound of the crackling road. Dad didn't laugh. He just cleared his throat and drove the truck.

Visors blocked out the afternoon sun. The rifle barrels glimmered like halos on a gun rack above my head. As we got closer I could smell the river through the sealed windows of the truck. Such power. Facing down the gun seemed worth it just to see those steel monsters' farts propelling them through the great river. I imagined them alive working in communion with the men on board.

As Dad and Pat unloaded the rifles, I jumped from the truck and ran with anticipation. Rain boots hit the grass and stopped. A white slab of wood laid on the lawn next to the lighthouse. Empty inside except some cobwebs. Whatever worked it long gone.

Breathless, I turned back to the river. Another freighter was approaching. A huge fart rippled across the water. Badass.

My Mom Gives Me a Little Tree From the Car Freshner Factory Where She's Worked for Seventeen Years

She tells me it's scented wrong.
"We can't use it."

It says Evergreen but smells like Black Ice.
My car smells like bile.
I can use this.

Little Trees

sometimes
I stop into Sunoco
for a Rockstar
and impulse buy
a Little Tree
as if a little whiff
reconnects me
with home

Car Freshner

When Julius Samann
fled the Nazis
he found himself
in Watertown
and in 1952
he invented
Little Tree
air fresheners
and the first thing
he said after
inventing
New Car Smell
was fuck it
I'm calling this company
Car ~~Freshener~~
Freshner

So Many Little Trees

Hanging
new trees
over
each dulled
and scentless
old tree
planting
a tiny forest
in my rearview.

Kendra

When I was ten
I found $3 on the ground
that I used to buy
a Spider-Man comic
off a spinner rack
at Tiny's General Store
across from the cemetery

Two days later
my sister Kendra
who was four at the time
got mad at me for something
I don't remember
and ripped up
that Spider-Man comic book

I am 34 writing a poem
Spider-Man is a bunch
of famous actors
I haven't seen a spinner rack
in years and Kendra has three kids
but we don't talk much anymore.

Roads to the Future are Paved with the Fists of Loved Ones

You've lost count how many times your kid brother's been to jail but you remember vividly the one time you open-palm slapped his face, the way it changed color, shape, the curdling of soft skin and the tears that flowed, and how you understood it really is possible to change the course of time with one trivial act.

It didn't take a journey.

Timeshare

When I was about seven or eight my family had taken a vacation to Disney World. I know I was very young because my sister was still a baby. Anyway, I guess to save some money my father had figured on attending one of those timeshare breakfasts. Where they give you discount tickets to the parks for attending their pitch. Being very young and seeing the roadside outlets – storefronts shaped like tropical fruit, colonial ships, and mouse ears – I got a little too excited on the way to breakfast. There are kids, I thought, real kids, who get to live here all the time. When was Mickey Mouse, a likely face around the neighborhood, going to jump out and greet me? When would we see the grand finale? Is it really about the journey? This place we'd arrived at, this was just a parking lot.

"Breakfast?" I whined into the blistering bright morning, my voice echoing over the vehicular sea, "I can't wait through breakfast! Tower of Terror!" His monstrous mitts grabbed hold of my arm, a twig not yet a bicep, and the bloodshot old man stifled a throaty growl through his teeth, "the *fuck-ing ba-by* is *slee-ping*!" We checked on my infant sister still snoozing, soundly strapped into her car seat.

I can't recall now when the bruise formed. Just the color, this warped watercolor of yellows and blues. Sometimes I think about it. Now that I'm grown I do things I'm ashamed of and there's a mark, a totem I guess, keeping me on guard. And that thing seems to always be there. Little things.

Following me. Staring. Look at me, the imprint on my finger says when I mysteriously lose my wedding band. Look at me, my wide eyes say after briefly nodding off at the wheel. I'm not going away, the shame says even after I'm once again wearing the band. Even after I'm startled awake by shrieking steel guardrail. I'm always looking out, spinning the tungsten band on my finger or looking in the rearview. When you're a child you don't realize all these secret items people carry with them. I wonder what symbol of shame my father carried around that park all week, as it followed him, holding his hand. What he felt when I stepped before that ginormous silver globe and raised my glowing arm to the azure sky.

So anyway, he bought that timeshare after all.

Well, This is Fucking Clever

you're not going to believe this
but there's actually a factory
at the intersection
of Factory Street and Mill Street
and it's a paper mill
a burned-out brick shell
with grids of broken glass
overlooking the river
that I would think
was abandoned
if I didn't
sometimes notice
the *Days Without Accident*
sandwich board sign
go back to <u>0</u>.

Jackie

I was walking
and looking at the ground
to avoid tripping
over raises and dips
in the sidewalk
when a girl pulled up
in a rust-pocked Ford Explorer
she had a smoker's rasp
and she said her name was Jackie
and she asked if I remembered her
and she said we kissed
five years ago
and she asked if I remembered now
sorry Jackie.
I still don't remember.
this is embarrassing.

A Warm Rain Falls Outside the Municipal Arena After the Watertown Wolves Scored the Winning Goal During Overtime

Hollowed out
by the thought
that I may never again
experience
the blistering pain
of a Lake Ontario
blizzard
whipping
my stupid face
till it's numb.

Bummer.
Thought there'd be snow.
Cool to see the home team win though.

The Tragically Hip

Canada is an open wound
bleeding maple syrup
and Labatt Blue
into America
and the only way
to know
where the bleeding ends
is when you stop
hearing
The Tragically Hip
on the radio.

Interview with the Sandwich Assassin

...

Too many jobs, man. You'd shit if you knew how many. Well, I lost count but you'd need to take a sock off, at least.

...

Oh, best I ever had? Easy. Place in Watertown called Jreck Subs. Me and the boys would get drunk or stoned in the walk-in and it made the whole customer service thing go a lot smoother. Fuckin' K-ROCK was playin' "New Orleans is Sinking" by The Hip on the radio like every hour. Those guys kicked ass. Everyone who worked at Jreck's loved their shit. They were like the middle ground where stoners and jocks met up to chill. We'd craft a bowl out of, like, some foil and pens or a tomato corer or something. Sometimes we shoved our fists into the tuna salad, shuddering at the cold shredded slop running through our fingers. One time this dude Chase fucked his girl in the cooler. It was awesome.

...

Unsanitary? Shit naw, we wore gloves. Come on, we weren't perverts.

...

Customers? Haha, customers loved us. They came in and we sprang into action like a fuckin' ballet. The way I smoothly sliced open a roll with a swipe of a bread knife, whipping meats and cheeses onto the sandwich with the nimble fingers of a blackjack dealer, it was cool as shit. We were sub shop ninjas, man. Played games with customers, too, like Blind Kid and New Kid.

...

Well, they were essentially the same game. There'd be two of us working. Someone was the always the new kid or the blind kid and the other was the regular kid. See, the blind kid couldn't see anything. New kid just didn't know where anything was.

...

Hell yeah, they got pissed. We'd just smile and hook 'em up with some free shit, cookies, extra large drinks and what not. People love free shit and I figure it's worth it to put up with a couple of goons bustin' yer balls, right? Most of the time they didn't give a shit though. You see someone havin' a good time at a shit job and you aren't going to make a thing out of it This girl Carol lived across the street from Jreck's so sometimes she'd come in and we'd hook her up with a meal. My boys would come in so of course they'd eat free. It felt good, providing for people without expectation of something in return. I read somewhere it boosts your Oxycontin levels or whatever.

...

Oh, right, the manager. Sure, he got a little pissed off from time to time. Usually we'd point out all the times he got wasted with us and did the same thing. Then he'd drop it. Besides, apart from giving everything away for free, we were too good at our jobs to be replaced. Sandwich assassins. Anyway, that dude, he was busy studying to take the cop test. I hear he's doing real well on the force, workin' his way up the chain. Makes sense. If anyone'd make a cool cop it's him.

...

So , I know it ain't really chill to discuss how much money you make but let's just call it $6.35. An hour. I was eighteen so I didn't care. A future wasn't something I had in mind.

...

Most of those guys left for college and my mom said I had to get a real job and move out so I guess my tenure at Jreck's had to come to an end, too. For a while I thought I loved it because we were always getting drunk and stoned, which ruled. Then, like, I've had plenty jobs that I got drunk and stoned at and they still sucked. Gig I got now, drivin' forklift at 84 Lumber, gave me tennis elbow from pullin' levers all day. Can you imagine? Tennis elbow. From a forklift. There ain't nothin' like eight hours of simple movement to remind you about loneliness. Anyway, I think I just liked being around people I have shit in common with uniting against a common enemy like customers or making sandwiches while chill music plays on an old radio. Commie, uh, karma-whatchamacallit.

...

Camaraderie, right. For that little bit of time it felt like our own camaraderie space Some nights we wouldn't even leave right away. We'd close up and pick out a booth and shoot the shit over cards. Poker. Show me a job anyone loves enough to not rush out the door when the clock stops. So, if yer writin' a book about Watertown, you should put that in it.

...

Couple years back, the owner got busted doin' some shady shit and the government seized their assets. Bedazzlement or whatever. Whatta idiot.

...

I still love their food though. I go in sometimes and I see it changing. They sell pizza and chicken wings now. A sub shop, selling pizza. Now they got sailboat wheels and fishnets on the wall and shit like yer at fuckin Applebee's. Back when I was there, we had nothin but a broken clock on the wall.

...

Wait, what kinda book is it anyway?

...

Oh. Sounds kinda gay. No offense.

Fat

I think if I moved
back to Watertown
I could finally settle down
and let myself become fat.

A Life's Total Value: $36.75

Fishtailed my car
on black ice
on the road
on the way
to work
narrowly avoiding
another car
I could have died
but I made it
and I made
$7.35 an hour
for five hours work
and when I finished
I got in my car
and drove
sliding
in the snow
for an hour.

Finding Immortality Inside Cheap Paper Cups of Powdered Hot Cocoa

Twenty-four hour
Sunoco stations lighting
uneven asphalt streets

an endless throat
dry swallowing
bleeding inside out

Chuck Taylors trudging
through knee-deep snow
freezing to death as competition

snow rising
last Tetris levels fast
consuming all travelers

Childhood Neighborhood

contemplated my own mortality
and memory
when confronted
by faded paint
and lack of activity
entire houses
reduced to plots of gravel.
hard to confess
to someone you love
that you've actually had fun here
and you're entirely capable
of doing it again.

PBBJ

Horror movies and peanut butter. My parents were never home after school so I'd waddle my little doughy body to the blue house next door. Our neighbor Ralph, the fifty-something John Lennon lookalike, didn't mind. He'd taped all the *Nightmare on Elm Street*s and he made a mean peanut butter and jelly. I found out later it was plain old butter that he'd lightly toasted onto each slice before spreading the main ingredients, which melted onto the still-warm Wonder Bread. Clouds of Jif creamy crawled through the dirty house, clawing its way to me as I sat before a box TV set and a coffee table littered with beer cans. The charred movie murder villain made his move before tracking-jumps made a victim out of the cassette. Ralph's daughter Sally was my age. She would come by from her mother's for a few hours and we'd eat PBBJs and play with her WWF action figures. She had Bret "The Hitman" Hart on her wall and her dad got her into the Beatles by playing old records. PBBJ is for fast kids with busy parents. Careless. My mom called me a few years ago to tell me Sally died. Ralph's back went bad and his house faded and chipped to a dulled gray. VHS bit the dust and so did the thing that came after it. If I open a thing of Country Crock and the Jif jar, maybe I can fire up the stove and bring it all back.

Concerned Whether I Genuinely Love This Place or If I Am Romanticizing Poverty Through These Poems

Just a slight jerk
of the shoulder
and a curled lip
as she passes
a little gesture
to impress
a nonexistent high society

I sincerely love
every
single
cigarette
stuck
in sidewalk cracks
and every
pregnant butt
in Tweety Bird
sweatpants
pushing a stroller
through the snow
and every shred
of duct tape
over bullet holes
in the Great American
Supermarket's
windows

I only feign ironic
detachment
in order
to pass myself off

as a functioning
human
being.

Racing Against Ghosts

Steve came stumbling off the curb in cargo shorts and a polo shirt. Swung open the door and fell in shotgun, a movement so fluid I thought he'd rehearsed it. Sweating booze, he leaned over and put a tongue in my ear like it was supposed to be sexy.

"Not here," I said, looking around to make sure no one saw us.

He belched and the stench of Bud Light bloomed throughout my Taurus.

"Jesus." But who was I to judge? I was drunk, too. Looked around craning my neck from side to side. Not a body in sight, only darkness and a couple yellow porch lights. Coast clear. So I floored it.

"Whoa!"

Steve pressed his hand against the dashboard.

"Welcome to the Batmobile, baby."

Steve laughed.

"This *is* the fuckin' Batmobile!"

Shit, why did I say baby?

Steve came home from SUNY Potsdam for summer. I didn't go to college. I got a job working at the Car Freshner plant. A puncher. You know the little hole where the string gets tied at the top of the Little Trees? Well, I'm the guy who punches that hole with a piston machine. All day I'm punching and sending them by the crateful over to the guy or girl who'll be stringing.

He had a beard, too. Everyone was growing beards. I couldn't grow one so I told people I thought shaving was manlier. Dragging razors across my face, hell yeah.

I was speeding down Flower Ave by the golf course, looking for a good spot when I saw a familiar face in a passing car. Whoever it was, we made eye contact for a second and I was sure he recognized me. Fuck. Don't turn around and follow me. Maybe if I get it up to sixty they'll forget they saw me and not turn around.

"Why are we going so fast?"

"I saw someone."

"Who?"

"Zach, I think."

"Zach who?"

"I think his name's Zach."

"Zach?"

"The lacrosse player, Zach."

"All lacrosse players are named Zach."

Headlights winked in the dark behind me like they were saying, we know all about you, dude.

We know and we're comin' to gitcha! When you're living a secret life, every passing car, every stranger's glance, every shadow cast has the potential to expose you.

I parked us in the lot of a funeral home several miles outside city limits. Red lights from the radio tower in a nearby field flashed across a stretch of darkened road.

I got out of the car and kicked some gravel and took a long pull from a bottle of Yukon Jack. Steve got close and breathed into my lips. "What was that all about? Driving like that?"

He peeled my shirt from my skin getting his hands underneath, kissed my gritty neck, and I dropped the bottle next to the tire hearing some of it slosh out into the dirt. Guys always kiss like they already own you, like they don't care if you break apart in their mouths. He pulled me close by the button of my jeans, tearing them open.

"Sorry," I said. "I just don't want anyone to know."

"Trust me," he whispered between kisses, "everyone already knows."

"What?"

"Maybe I had too much to drink and said something?" He stepped back and I could sense his shame in the darkness, standing there all hairy chest and stooped shoulders.

"Are you mad?"

I leaned against the hood of the car looking down. Avoiding eye contact, absorbing his confession. Probably could have taken him. Even just a sucker punch. I thought about getting inside my car and gassing it back to town, leaving him stranded half naked at the funeral home on an empty back road. I thought about the ways to ruin him. Ah, fuck.

My chapped throat burned. Feeling my gut wring itself out of booze and betrayal, I swallowed it down. Then I stood up and pulled him back to me. Everyone wants to play the tough guy in heartbreak.

We traded swigs for a couple hours looking up at the blinking lights over the radio tower before passing out in the backseat beneath a used beach towel.

Last I heard, Steve's married and manages a bar down in Myrtle Beach. Me, I'm still punching away. Not mad about what happened between us. Not anymore. Goddamn.

Frederick Exley

Watertown's oldest restaurant
is The Crystal
there is a sign out front
that used to say

cRystal
restaurant

but now
the lights are broken.

The black tile
around the entrance
is chipping
exposing the stucco.

Frederick Exley
would get drunk
at the Crystal
and bitch about
the Buffalo Bills
and how he should
be famous.
He wrote about it
in *A Fan's Notes*
back when
the tile was fresh.
He's been dead
since '92.
Watertown's
forgotten
author.

I'm not trying
to be remembered
or talk about football.
I just go to the Crystal
to eat eggs.

A Nostalgia Problem

Oh, I've got a nostalgia problem?
This whole fuckin town's got
a nostalgia problem, pal.
You got two bars called
Flashback Lounge and Time Warp Tavern
on the same street
separated by nothin'
but two blocks
of dilapidated houses
meth kitchens
feral cat basements
and a church
and both bars smell
like burnt oil and Marlboro Reds
and suddenly
I've got the fuckin' nostalgia problem?
Fuck you.
Get the fuck outta my office.

First Kiss

Recalling my first kiss
when I was fifteen
with a girl named Ashleigh
who taught me how to huff Lysol
with a washcloth
over the top
of the aerosol can
after watching Empire Records.
We sat on her front porch
and I pulled up my JNCO's
so it didn't look like I was
wearing a denim skirt on each leg
and Ashleigh said
"do it like this
like a little kitty cat drinking milk
and not like a dog that's hungry."
It tasted like
a pine tree public swimming pool
from the Lysol on my lips
but only a little.
Kitties don't need to drink so much.

you should write a poem about me

my mom didn't let us have books in the house when i's a kid. one time comin' home after school with some libary books she slapped me so hard i dropped 'em and she goes "think yer smart, huh? think yer fuckin better'n me?" before i even got my snowpants off. now i still can't read for shit. sometimes i still miss her.

you should put that in yer book.

Nostalgia is a form of grieving. Being in love is to be nostalgic for the present.

Friends Back Home

Kyle sent me a PornHub link
and said
check it out haha.
I like to laugh
so I checked it out.
A blonde girl in a car
gave an enthusiastic blowjob
to a faceless guy
she held his come in her mouth
while she walked into the mall.
I knew the Gander Mtn
the food court
and the place that sells wicker furniture
and hand-carved signs that read
a messy kitchen is a happy kitchen
the girl sat down on a bench
swallowed
smiled for the camera.

Many of the commentors
also knew the mall
I used to sit on that bench.
That's my hometown mall.
I live in Watertown right now
please let me fuck you.
PornHub user analthrust95 said
i used to shop at that gander
Wow
I guess a lot of people
from Watertown
are on PornHub.

The point I'm getting at is
I hope you someday

get to experience the thrill
of seeing
something you love
have its moment
portrayed in a movie
or a book
or a sex act posted on PornHub
but not so often
that it feels dull and overexposed.

No, what I'm really saying is
I want you to have a friendship
comfortable and intimate enough
to share porn
together
shamelessly.

Boat Dream

you told me
to take you
on another boat
tour along
the river
among the islands
but if I had
my way we
would never
have gotten
off the first
one

a town called gravity

we said
Watertown
was like
gravity

people would escape
their rural roots
for better things only
to return soon after

we forgot that
escaping gravity
means falling
forever

doing this poetry thing about Watertown.
Real jerkoff shit.
one I'm doing now is about The Hitch

Dan

my only real memory of the Hitchin Post is
one time we went there, you told me [my
girlfriend] was cheating on me, while she
and the guy she was cheating with were
standing right there

Kevin

Hitchin Post

there is a dive bar called the hitchin post
that is dog shit brown outside
dark inside
and all the characters
have scars
and limps
and missing teeth
my friends and i went there ironically
because it seemed like a place
where people get hurt
but
irony repeated enough
becomes truth.

secret to living in a small town

let me tell you
the secret to living
in a small town is
to acknowledge that
everyone you've loved
has shared intimacies
with someone else
you know and
these connections exist
at the intersections of
a shining inescapable web
never to be pulled apart

jettison jealousy upon entry
welcome to the fuck web.

we're taking a road trip to the city

get in
we're going to the city
that's right, motherfucker

Syracuse.

Seen By Appointment Only

Walking around
Watertown I observed
a realty sign in front of
a small prefabricated house
the sign read
I'M GORGEOUS INSIDE
to which I softly
whispered
"me too."

If You Travel Far Enough North You End Up in the South Again

near the St Lawrence River
in a pickup truck's rear window
a confederate flag decal
or the rebel flag
whatever it's called
so faded and smoker's yellow
that it could almost be denied
existence at all
as if time had rendered this
statement null
ineffective
or as if the person who
placed it there never truly
cared at all

Local Celebrity

Growing up in a small town, I find it's even more exciting when someone local is able to break through and find success on a major platform. I first experienced this sensation as a boy.

When I was eleven I was ashamed of my little penis so I got my parents to take me to the doctor. Doctor said, "It's not small, you're just fat." Well, he didn't say I was fat, just that there was "a lot of fat."

Months later, Shawn Michaels underwent back surgery leading up to *Wrestlemania XIV*. It was in an interview segment – "there he is!' I pointed at the TV. There he was working on Shawn Michaels' back. Dr. Vasquez, the man who looked at my tiny penis.

Ode to People That Never Left Their Shitty Hometowns For a Tiny Overpriced Apartment in a Major City

A hometown is not
a prison or place
to escape from
It isn't holding you back
It's nothing
a geographic crapshoot
a name on a map ready to burn
It's a place you can
bury your demons
or dig them up
and dance
for a night or forever
You can stay or leave
Doesn't really matter.

Needs Citation

Richard Grieco is
originally from Watertown
shit, you can find that on Wikipedia
but Wikipedia won't tell you how
after *21 Jump Street* ended
Richard Grieco came back
on a bender
and stole some kid's bicycle
and joy rode it all over town.
Someone else
told me that story
and now I've been trying
to add it
to Richard Grieco's Wikipedia page,
If you are a verified Wikipedia editor
please contact me
my email is
daniel.rh.eastman@gmail.com.

Clippers

The old man's barber pole was in the shape of a lighthouse out front of the Clipper Barbershop. You'd go in through a door in the back, up a darkened ramp with an aquarium lit up along the wall. He had those suck fishes and some goldfish the size of a baseball glove and some others that glowed electric blue. Kids could press their faces against the glass and he didn't seem to give a shit. In the room with the red chair all pumped up there were these nautical trinkets: replica ships, nets, hooks, hundred-year-old black-and-white photos of men in slickers smoking corn cob pipes. He still wore a white smock like the old days. He'd cough over you and scratch his stubbly white face. If you were six or sixty you'd come out of the chair the same: short on top, even shorter on the sides and tapered in the back. When he died they tore it down and threw up a Tilted Kilt so guys who felt powerful after selling used cars could go drink beer and ogle cleavage in those German girl dresses the Kilt servers wear. Hey, did you know clipper is what they call the hair trimmers and also the name for an old sailing ship? Fuck, man, that was a nice pun.

Lighthouse Man

In my dreams
I am a superhero
I am Lighthouse Man
with a big-ass
lighthouse
growing
out of the top
of my head

Scanning the world
telling those
in the distance to
keep away
keep back
or risk
shipwrecking
on my shores

Just cruise
your own way

I am Lighthouse Man
in my dreams
When I wake
I'm just
a regular joe
with an odd-shaped skull

Love Poem

I want a marriage that opens like French doors with broken locks in the dead of winter.

I want a love like a first date in a sticky dive: Everyone around us 30 years older so we finish our single drink and drive home capping the evening with an awkward hug. None of this is what we'd expected.

I want sex like a SWAT team splintering the kitchen door to a crack den with a battering ram, slamming all inhabitants face down before they know what's happening. It goes on for minutes before they realize there never were any drugs. This is simply how we live.

Fish Eye

There was this guy on the north side of town born with a fucked up eye problem where he always looked out the sides of his head. These dudes who worked at the paper mill used to drive by in their big metal trucks and yell "Hey, Fish Eye!" So everyone called him Fish Eye. He'd hang around the general store and garage where I'd go rent Chucky movies. I remember him, sort of. He came in with his hunched back and fucked up eyes wearing this dirty brown bomber jacket. I remember thinking, So, this is the guy. The lady at the counter, Brenda, had no neck and talked with a goose honk in her voice. She called me Danny and she called Fish Eye by his real name, whatever it was. Outside the store one day, the guys rolled up in the big truck and the dude in the passenger seat yelled "Hey Fish Eye!" with a laugh but they got caught at a red light just then. Fish Eye saw a chance and took off running. Leaping onto the runners of the truck, he gripped the passenger side mirror and started wailing wildly on the guy inside. Those paper guys didn't know what the fuck. Driver couldn't figure whether to laugh or panic. And the passenger's just trying to keep from getting his face blasted. Punches were erratic, no real control over his arms. Not like a guy who knows how to throw a punch. More like his crazy ass didn't even know he'd just hopped onto a moving truck. One eye focused on the target of his erratic punches. The other watched itself in the mirror, triumphant.

So, that was the guy.

Semi-Pro

Watertown is home to the Red & Black, the oldest semi-pro football team in the US, founded in 1896. I'm trying to figure out what to do with this knowledge since I was never into football. I liked to drink and I got a DUI. My memory of this team is, like, huge dudes bowling over one another in snow-slick grass in the middle of November.

Semi-pro. The name alone it ensures participants a lifetime of obscurity. It's like being partially-pro, somewhat-pro, not-quite-pro, or incomplete-pro. It reeks of insignificance. As if anything less than the mountaintop is a waste of potential. Either go full pro or be a fucking loser forever. I don't know, man. We've each got our own mountain. Going into a semi-pro field presupposes the knowledge that what you are doing is less than. So the only logical explanation for your participation is love.

Okay, but look. I did know this guy named John – or maybe it was Jon – John something who played for the Red & Black but stopped when his daughter was born and he started managing a Price Chopper grocery store. I liked John. John Leblonsky. Called him the Big Leblonsky. Always laughed at my suicide jokes. In my mind he's still this 6'5" 350lbs monster who has to walk through doors sideways and always looks dirty like he just got done working on a huge truck. Ran into him in the Price Chopper once and he was wearing this bright white shirt that outshined the fluorescent lights. That's when I asked him if he was still playing football. Sort of shook his head half-hearted like "nah." I asked if he missed it and he kinda shrugged and said, "ahh, sometimes, but I got a kid now." And that, he said, is the best thing that ever happened to him. Then he looked past me and onto the next recyclable face in the line. See, love never ends but it can be put into competition with new love. And I think that counts. It totally counts. Hell yeah, John. Keep on shinin' my dude.

Watertown is Home to Fort Drum and the 10th Mountain Division, the Most Deployed Unit in the US Military Since 2001

Sometimes you're going to run into trouble. Returned-home soldiers in camo pants, high and tights, and faces peppered with 3am shadows glaring at me from across a crowded trailer. Their shoulders are widened from thousands of pushups and months of carrying assault packs. Girls hold them back. "You know what you did," I see one mouth at me. In various states of blacking out it could have been anything. Someone else whispers in my ear, "He's just drunk and looking to fight." I am wearing baggy jeans and a hoodie. I haven't had a haircut. I stumble straight back to a kitchen and pull a steak knife. It will be self-defense. I am drunk and expecting a fight. There is shouting in the next room coming for me. A different girl leads me to a door. There are stairs behind it. This is no trailer. I am locked in the basement with a steak knife. There are a few kids playing XBOX here. I sit on a plaid couch. I don't know what I did. Could have been anything. I am a whirlwind of chaos striking madness into the hearts of US Army soldiers. I stab the knife into a couch cushion and pass out. When I awaken it is morning and everything is flooded with light. The fog of war has lifted. I like to think of myself as mostly harmless. Shaky on my feet but feeling like a winner. I find my way clear across a few bodies and into my car. I start it up and spew a rancid yellow streak across the steering wheel.

No One Remembers Him Anyway

A Toyota Tercel skids
to a stop at a red light on
Washington Street by the
Roswell P. Flower Memorial Statue.
He was a politician or something.
No one remembers him anyway.

His statue is simply
there.
Dividing the intersection.

A faint glow emerges from the shrubbery.
A boy of sixteen stumbles forth
carrying a flip phone in front of his face.

The driver of the Tercel thinks
"that guy is drunk," and feels
a sense of danger in her belly.
"Hey, I'm drunk too," she thinks.
"But not like that."

The boy screams into the phone,
"You know where you are?
Yer in the jungle baby!
You gonna die!"
He cackles at this.

Green light fades to life.
The Tercel's motor buzzes
the tires swerve
on the slick asphalt.
Into a nearby backyard

the boy disappears.

Watertown

Watertown is
a huge ass
and the crack is
the Black River
running down
the middle

because it looks like shit
and smells

Touchhole

Carol's dad was halfway through a box of Franzia when Kevin and I walked into the kitchen. He was always halfway through a box of Franzia in the kitchen.

"Hey, touchholes," he said as he hung up the phone on the wall. It was a term of endearment, like dickhead or cocksucker or shit fer brains. "You finish college?"

Kevin nodded and smirked like he hadn't graduated two years prior.

Carol's dad looked at me. He looked like a pre-shotgun Hemingway. "How bout you? You finish college?"

"College? Nah," like I was above that shit. "I ain't going to college. I'm gonna move to California and write."

Carol's dad had his living room lined with shelves of old books. He'd read everything.

"Writing?"

"I figure I don't need a degree for that."

"Haha, a writer. You don't wanna be a writer. You just wanna sit on the beach and watch the cunt go by. Why else would you go to California? If you were a writer you'd write something right now."

Carol's dad had read everything so if anyone would know. He nodded to the phone hanging on the receiver.

"Just got off the phone about her college loans. You're right not to go. Shit's expensive."

"Is she upstairs?"

"In her room, yeah."

Long solemn walk up twelve wooden steps with a bottle of Arbor Mist. Creaking like little yawns.

Yawn.
Yawn.
Yawn.
Yawn.
Yawn.
Yawn.
Yawn.
Yawn.
Yawn.
Yawn.
Yawn.
Yawn.

He was right about me. Expensive had nothing to do with it. I had no ambition. He saw right through me. I was going to drown. Swallowed up by a flood of shit water. I'd never wanted to leave Watertown more than I did then and I knew more than ever that I never would.

Barry Freed in Reverse

Of course I will occasionally imagine
myself a villainous alter ego
polluting the Saint Lawrence River
just to give my ordinary self
something to save.

Carthage 52 Watertown 26

ain't lookin' good folks
we got a chilly 13 degrees
under floodlights tonight

once again
high school football rivalries
refusing to keep it on the field
numb knuckle freezing
bleachers bleeding fistfights

them farm boys must be putting something in the
   water up there

Growing Up Without Money Never Really Felt Traumatic to Me

bury me in a
mausoleum made of
outdated wood paneling
finger-stained floral wallpaper patterns

make my coffin
a claw foot tub
preserved with walled stacks
of waterlogged VHS tapes

send me back there

piss off the neighbors
remodel the broken home
flip it for a profit

Just an Old Black Man Trying to Find His Way Home

I park in the lot behind the Flower Library. Every house here looks like it could be a dive bar. Maybe every dive bar looks like poor people housing. The Solar Building's got bricks falling off and tile torn up like an earthquake hit it and they fucked off like it'd better off if they didn't fix it. She's up there waiting for me on the third floor. The top floor. There's the stairwell or the creaky Art Deco cage elevator. Pack of Kools crushed underfoot. I'm nineteen and she's twenty-one going on forty-seven with a smoker's lung. Her husband is in Iraq. Or Afghanistan. One of those. I've been cheated on. I want to see what it's like on the other side. There's a kind of badge of honor in it being a married woman, a sense of superiority in claiming another man's territory. We met at the call center we both work at inside the old Woolworth's. She offered to buy me a case of Labatt's and I took it as a sign.

Midnight's orchestra cranks up. A screen door crashes shut. A voice calls to me, "Young man. Young man." I am trapped in his sights on the alley street between the library lot and the Solar Building. "Young man, can ya spare some change?"

Fuck, I was just trying to go have sex. I want to fuck a married woman. "Come on, man," he rasps, cigarette in hand. "I just need five, ten, or fifteen dollar man." His spastic arm waves the dart like a victory flag. "Five, ten, or fifteen dollars. Come on, man!"

"I ain't got no money, sorry."

There's a light on up there. Could it be her? Is she seeing this? He grabs my t-shirt pulling my attention back. Is she look down here seeing what a pussy ass bitch I'm being?

"I'm tryna be yer friend, man! I'm just an old black man tryna find my way home!" He's so desperate. The cigarette waves too close to my face. I give him a shove.

"Watch the fuckin cigarette, dude."

He flicks into the breeze. I imagine a hiss. "Don't worry about it."

Click. The blade appears turning the fist into a rattlesnake.

Fuck, I'm going to die tonight, huh? I'm going to bleed out for some pussy. Shit, put that on a t-shirt. "BLEED OUT FOR PUSSY".

"I said I'm tryna be yer friend. Five, ten, fifteen dollars..."

Fuck.

"No, thanks."

He's still pacing a circle under the streetlight when I peel out. I hear him calling out. "Shit fuck shit fuck."

I drive around Public Square several times appreciating being alive and not stabbed. I think about how I'm going to be better. I have my whole life ahead of me. Life is too delicate just to go around taking it for granted. Any turn of chance can —

I park on a curb down the block and jog up to the Solar Building. I know she's still up there waiting for me. I mean, come on. I'm not stupid.

Tore a Hole in the Fabric
of Reality

while sipping coffee
on a porch made of two by fours
wearing a white t-shirt
turned mustard yellow
and basketball shorts
meditating on an oil stain
in the driveway

reflected back
an image
of myself
clean cut
expensive clothing
working not hard
in a sanitized box

before my next sip swallowed
the universe sewed itself
back together

You Loved It When We Were Kids. What Happened?

I bought an old box TV set from the pawnshop. It doesn't turn on but I thought we could take it down to the rock quarry and smash it like old times. It's even got the wood grain on the sides and back. These new flat screens, they just don't do it for me. Come on!

A Poem About Friendship

As a kid, your best friend's house reeked of cigarette smoke and burnt cheese but they always had the coolest action figures and video games.

As a teenager, your best friend's house was stainless with plenty of natural light and you thought this was maybe how rich people lived.

As an adult, your house is a cramped studio you can't afford and you don't have friends.

Hell

I don't think it's really all fire and pain like they say. I think everyone's got their own thing coming. I dunno. My version of Hell? Well, my dick's still there. The sun's shining over the lake. Temp's a comfy 75 during the day but drops to a cool 60 at night. We build bonfires out of dry branches when the sun goes down. Everyone I've ever loved is with me. Every friend. Hell, even some enemies too. We take the boat out sometimes or we just sit back in Adirondack chairs. We drink but we never get drunk. Cheap beer in an endless cooler. We're forever in that sweet spot right after the first or second drink when your belly gets warm and you can talk about anything. Sleep is optional. Night comes, we share a furnished cabin with those green 70s countertops and pine needles in the carpet. Someone always plays some half decent guitar. We circle the fire and listen to owls and the hush rippling of the shore. A column of smoke reaches the stars and all of our secrets are carried away and dissolved. Still, in spite of the eternal beauty of earthly nature and leisure at our disposal, none of us can escape the unspoken feeling that this is not enough.

That Celebration in the Getaway Car Right Before the Big Climax

When tax brackets are prisons
one is born into
every minute spent outside
rural county lines
feels like the joyride scene
between breakout and recapture

U-Haul Truck

She had her ashy, chapped heels up on the dashboard of the U-Haul truck. She had slipped her torn, tattered Chuck Taylors on the floor of the U-Haul truck. Olive-toned, tatted up, bicycle thighs rode high in the August breeze of the U-Haul truck. Skin-deep symbols of self-expression extended from her knees to her feet in a U-Haul truck. Me with my stained, plain white tee and cargo shorts in the driver's seat of a U-Haul truck. Bare legs sweated and stuck to pleather interior of a U-Haul truck. Unseen were the forever marks we gave to one another in a U-Haul truck. It was an older model, boxy with low-throttle, no CD player, no adapter, just a burned-out tuner, only static between the two of us, in a U-Haul truck. Oh, the radio silence of a U-Haul truck. Six hours is a long way with nothing to say to an ex-friend and an old flame in a U-Haul truck. Former consorts, now nonconcentric, found a means to their ending in a U-Haul truck. We had packed up and strapped our belongings in the back, locked down that ratcheted latch of a U-Haul truck. Most of the haul was hers – collections of books, mostly unread, records, and ephemera – in the U-Haul truck. I, on the other hand, had my own motives, always ready to go without notice, just a stack of clothes and a bag to tote it in a U-Haul truck. And now it's her and me and these catalytic rumblings, refusing to be muffled in a U-Haul truck. That summer was so hot, man, the heat was oppressive, I was running a temper, I was hotheaded, I was aggressive, in a U-Haul truck. I gripped fistfuls of steering wheel and my tanned knuckles turned bleach white in a U-Haul truck. I kept turning to speak, seeking something to say in that U-Haul truck. We had hatchets to exhume and ice to break, in a U-Haul truck. Something about the way nothing brings people together like shared pain in a U-Haul truck, abandoning our together home and heading down opposite roads in a U-Haul truck. A languid drive had begun under a late-August sun in a U-Haul truck, ended at dusk, after three hundred and sixty miles of muted mouths and dials, opened up in a darkened lot unattended. Gutted. Unlocked. Empty.

Sure, I Know How to Swim. Why?

I am drifting on my back along the water.
Free-floating, I am driftwood.
I feel it clogging up my ears, sloshing in my brain.
I am drifting maybe to Canada, maybe to
  Heaven.
I'm in the main current now, relinquished all
  control.

Oh no, here come the rocks.

The Nice Side of Watertown

My wife points out the paint chipping off nearly every home we pass. I tell her it's vintage. She notes the lack any gainful employment opportunities here. I tell her it's got a quaint, small town feel.

I crank the wheel around a sharp corner overlooking the hill of vinyl homes, in-ground swimming pools, and an unoccupied golf course.

"Alright, now this is actually a nice part of Watertown," she says.

Still the same neighborhood it's always been. There's the blood-red tennis court.

There's a dad throwing down a push broom and whipping his son with a rusty bike lock for walking on the fresh-tarred driveway. Fuck. Oh fuck, he's really giving it to him.

Quick, turn this corner before she sees.

Acknowledgements

Special thanks to Cavin Gonzalez and Zac Smith for seeing a book out of these poems that started as jokes sent through email. Thank you to Katherine Eastman for putting up with Watertown. Lastly, thank you to my family and friends from back home and wherever you are now.

About the Author

Daniel Eastman is originally from Watertown, New York. That's basically Canada. He enjoys poutine and a good lake. Now he lives in Bethlehem, Pennsylvania where they used to make steel. Metal!

Read More from Back Patio Press!

Photographs of Madness: Inside Out
by Alec Ivan Fugate

I Could Be Your Neighbor, Isn't That Horrifying?
by Cavin Bryce Gonzalez

Time. Wow.
by Neil Clark

Venice
by TJ Larkey

NUMBSKULL
by No Glykon

A Completely Nonexistent Carnival
by Cavin Bryce Gonzalez

...and coming soon!

Good at Drugs
by KKUURRTT

Liver Mush
by Graham Irvin

Visit https://backpatio.press for more books
and online content. We love you all.

Thank you for reading.

– Cavin & Zac

Made in the USA
Coppell, TX
03 September 2022